A GIFT FOR:

....

FROM:

....

Copyright © 2016 Hallmark Licensing, LLC

Published by Hallmark Gift Books,
a division of Hallmark Cards, Inc.,
Kansas City, MO 64141
Visit us on the Web at Hallmark.com.

Editorial Director: Delia Berrigan
Editor: Kim Schworm Acosta
Art Director: Chris Opheim
Designer: Scott Swanson
Production Designer: Dan Horton
Writer: Keely Chace

ISBN: 978-1-63059-886-0
BOK1316

Made in China
1116

WELCOME HOME

INSPIRATION FOR THE PLACE YOU LOVE . . . AND LOVE TO SHARE

CONTENTS

WELCOME COME ON IN. STOP BY. DROP IN FOR A VISIT. SIT A SPELL. TAKE A LOAD OFF. PULL UP A CHAIR. PUT YOUR FEET UP. STAY AWHILE. TAKE IT EASY. MAKE YOURSELF AT **HOME.**

A WELCOME NOTE

Home. It's the place where we let our guard down and gather our loved ones. It's where we practice the fine art of hanging out and chipping in. It's where our shoes spill out from the closets and our memories shine out from the photos on the walls. It's the spot where we map out our dreams, and it's the dot that all our favorite GPS routes lead back to.

Like you, we at Hallmark put our hearts into our homes. We love sharing them with family and friends, but sometimes life—aka clutter, procrastination, lack of inspiration—gets in the way. So we asked our fellow moms, dads, artists, and home lovers to share their favorite ideas and best-loved tips for creating a space that is a meaningful expression of who they are—and leaves the chaos (mostly) at the door. We hope you'll feel inspired to love your home, and the people you share it with, even more.

COME IN

A great home has windows open to sunshine and doors open to friends.

NOTHING SAYS **WELCOME** LIKE A **SIGNATURE FLOURISH**

What distinctive touch would you use to identify your home for a first-time visitor? Maybe it's a seasonal wreath on the door. Maybe it's a three-foot butler statue named Tim who stands on your front step to greet guests. If you don't have a signature touch already, think about adding a little something that's meaningful and unique to you and your home.

FRAGRANT BLOOMS

Plant or pot flowers near your front door where not just the birds and bees can enjoy them! Peonies, roses, and lilies are popular choices, but do some research to see what will work best for your area and sun-shade conditions.

DO TRY THIS AT HOME

MAKE A LAUNCH PAD

Station a special cabinet, console, or small table near the door and make it your launch pad. Use it to hold everything that has to go out the door with you and your family in the morning: bags, wallets, keys, phone chargers . . . this should help you leave with everything on the first try!

Roll With It

Assign all family members their own wheeled bins so they can stash bags, shoes, and gear when they come home. Then, roll the bins back into the closet or under a bench.

Manage Your Mail

Mail with nowhere to go gets lost or quickly clutters up counters. Each day, after recycling junk mail, sort catalogs, magazines, bills, and "need to respond" items into baskets to go through when watching TV or after the kids are in bed. If you notice you never make time to look at certain subscriptions, cancel them.

A smile is always the most welcoming touch of all.

SCHEDULE A PARTY!

If you need a little extra organizing motivation, schedule a get-together at your home. Having that date in mind will keep you on track and give you a deadline. Better yet, you'll get to celebrate your hard work with people you love . . . and maybe even soak up some compliments!

Hierarchy of Home-Organizing Needs

EXPRESSION
A home that's a warm, welcoming reflection of you!

COMFORT
A peaceful, uncluttered haven where you can relax and recharge.

FUNCTION
A tidy domicile where you can find everything you
need and get out the door on time.

SAFETY
Things piled to the side or on tables to prevent tripping,
gouged feet, and general annoyance.

SHELTER
Roof over head, place to sleep, spot to put coffee
so it doesn't get ruined before you can drink it.

WHAT MAKES YOU HAPPY?

Ask yourself what you respond to in other homes or in that hotel you really loved on your last trip. What kinds of environments make you happy? Try to recreate that vibe in your own home:

- Bring that paint color you liked into your entry (or other area).
- Add the same kind of houseplant that made that other place feel so peaceful.
- Repurpose a vintage piece of furniture just like they did.
- Bring in wall art with a similar look, arrangement, or color palette.
- Shamelessly copy their clever storage ideas.

TIPS FROM OUR FURRY FAMILY MEMBERS

FOOD STORAGE

If you're just stashing my food bag, most any container will do. If you're pouring the food into the container, make sure it's food-safe.

Ditto.

TOYS

Keep some toys in a basket where I can get to them. Store the rest out of sight, and switch them out periodically.

Just wad up a piece of cluttery junk mail and toss it on the floor for me. Win-win.

WALKS

Oh, boy! Keep leash, harness, and waste bags on a hook by the door. Also, if there's room, put a small stool or bench by the door. It helps for putting my leash on, wiping my paws, and putting your own shoes on.

Do NOT attempt.

TREATS

Keep these handy in the front of a cabinet. I do love my treats!

I can climb high, dip into drawers, and open cabinets. You might as well just give them all to me now.

EMERGENCY INFO

Post vet and emergency vet numbers in an easy-to-read font in plain sight on the fridge or side of the fridge. Even better, have these numbers and addresses logged in your phone.

Ditto that.

ONE MORE THING...

You're awesome at creating a welcoming home, and I love you!

I was born knowing how to poop in a box. Clearly, I'm operating on a very high organizational level that you could probably learn from.

NOURISH

There's no such thing as too much laughter, too many fresh-baked chocolate chip cookies, or too much kitchen counter space.

TIDY-UP TUNES:
KITCHEN EDITION

"GREEN ONIONS"
by Booker T. & the MG's

"BREAD AND BUTTER"
by The Newbeats

"HONEY HONEY"
by ABBA

"MASHED POTATOES"
by Nat Kendrick & The Swans

"PEANUT BUTTER JELLY"
by Galantis

"POUNDCAKE"
by Van Halen

"YUMMY YUMMY YUMMY"
by Ohio Express

"HEY, GOOD LOOKIN'"
by Hank Williams

"POPCORN"
by Hot Butter

"COCONUT"
by Harry Nilsson

"HAM 'N' EGGS"
by A Tribe Called Quest

"I WANT CANDY"
by Bow Wow Wow

"STIR IT UP"
by Bob Marley

"LET'S CALL THE WHOLE THING OFF"
by Ella Fitzgerald and Louis Armstrong

"BEANS AND CORNBREAD"
by Louis Jordan and the Tympany Five

IF IT'S

- Broken
- Rusted
- Unused
- Unloved
- Missing pieces (especially lids without containers and vice versa)
- Duplicate or surplus*

REPURPOSE IT
DONATE IT
SELL IT
GIVE IT
TRASH IT

*Small and helpful duplicates like measuring cups and spoons can stay!

TIME FOR NEW (OR NEW TO YOU) DISHES?

WHY WHITE WINS

1 White dishes help your kitchen and dining area look cleaner and more peaceful.

2 They can make even boxed mac and cheese look gourmet.

3 It's easy to add to an all-white collection over time. New pieces won't need to come from the same set to look like they belong.

STORAGE SOLUTIONS TO LOVE

If you don't have a small fortune on hand for new cabinets, open up your kitchen and dining storage with one of these instead:

○ **A sideboard or hutch.** Not just for Grandma's china! Also great for appetizer plates, extra serving dishes, tea lights, votives with matches/lighter, birthday candles, flower vases, plasticware, and more.

○ **A thrift-store find or repurposed shelving unit.** Vintage goes with everything, and open shelves are perfect for showing off pitchers, vases, platters, and table linens.

○ **That hand-me-down baker's rack from a family member.** Make it yours by storing your own favorite dishes, cookbooks, baskets, and pieces of art on it.

○ **Wall-mounted racks, hooks, or magnet strips.** Keep mugs, pans, and utensils handy by storing them out in the open—on the wall. Bonus: It will make you look all chef-like.

If the scratches on our floors could talk, they'd say "fun was had here."

THERE IS A LOVE THAT HOLDS A FAMILY TOGETHER AND IT'S FOUND IN OUR HEARTS.

And there is a bottle of glue for everything else . . . It's found in the back of the kitchen junk drawer (90 percent sure).

3 FUN FRIDGE IDEAS

- **Meals-in-minutes baskets:** Put items that are used together in a basket. You could make a smoothie basket, with fruit, nuts, yogurt, and flaxseed, or a panini basket, with cheese, sliced meat, tomatoes, and condiments. It sparks ideas and saves time (and frustration).

- **Grab 'n' go for health:** Place healthy foods up front where you can see (and grab) them first, while relegating sugary options to the back. This works for pantry space, too, and it's great for helping kids and junk-food lovers of all ages choose a better alternative.

- **"Shelf of the week" strategy:** Cleaning the fridge can be an overwhelming to-do, so instead, designate a "shelf of the week." Take everything off the lucky shelf, purge anything that's expired, clean the shelf with warm soapy water, and wipe down the fridge walls around it. Bam...you're done!

Cool Notes

If you need to remind a family member about something important, put a sticky note INSIDE the refrigerator. They will see it—especially older kids and teens.

NOTHING SAYS **WELCOME** LIKE

FRESH-BAKED FRAGRANCE

To make your home smell like homemade cookies or cake, put a capful of vanilla in an ovenproof container and leave it in the oven for an hour at 275°F. Or try boiling a cinnamon stick in some water on the stove (but not for an hour!).

Family is
an endless
source of joy.
And dishes.

AT OUR TABLE, THERE'S ALWAYS ROOM FOR ONE MORE.

House + Love
= Home

A GREAT CONVERSATION IS A LITTLE BIT MAGICAL.

NOTHING SAYS **WELCOME** LIKE **COZY CONVERSATION SPACES**

- If you have a small family or opt more often for small, intimate get-togethers, then create a cozy space for one to three people to sit and talk.

- If you have a big family or regularly host large groups, you'll want to arrange a conversation area with as much seating as possible. Hint: Swivel chairs and no-back benches can do "double duty" as part of two seating areas at once.

- Whatever the number, there should be side tables for guests to place their drinks and plates.

ONLY PIRATES SHOULD BURY THEIR TREASURES. KEEP YOURS WHERE YOU CAN SEE THEM AND ENJOY THEM EVERY DAY.

Go Stylish With Storage

Especially in a smaller home without a catchall room or spare closet space, embrace the idea of storing things out in the open in decorative containers:

- Attractive baskets
- Vintage or other interesting boxes
- Big old bowls
- Apothecary jars
- Serving trays
- Storage ottomans
- Family heirloom vases
- Used candle containers (Wash out the old wax and voilà!)

Think about what you already have and love and what you could put in it. And when you're shopping in stores or online, keep your eye out for fun and pretty things that can be repurposed to hold stuff for you.

COLLAGE WALL 101

○ **GATHER** the items you want to collage. Go for a mix of family photos, three-dimensional wall art, framed art, kids art, and items representing different family members. Aim for a variety of colors, shapes, and sizes.

○ **EXPERIMENT** with the arrangement without committing to hammer and nails. Trace and cut out a paper stand-in for each collage item. Then, lay the paper stand-in on the back of the item and mark any nail hole locations on the paper, too.

○ **ARRANGE** and rearrange the paper stand-ins on your wall, using tape. You can keep your collage at eye-level or take it from floor to ceiling if you've got a lot to display.

○ **MARK** the wall when you're happy with the arrangement. Use a pencil to mark along the top, bottom, and sides of each paper stand-in. Take one nail and tap it lightly into each of the nail holes you've marked—just enough to pierce the paper and mark the needed nail or anchor locations on the wall.

○ **SWAP IN** the real collage items one at a time. Remove one paper stand-in and hammer in the needed nails (or install the anchors and screws) at the spot(s) you've marked. Then, hang the real thing.

DO TRY THIS AT HOME

LITTLE TOUCHES TO MAKE IT MEANINGFUL

Show Off Regional Pride!

If you grew up in a different state or country, celebrate treasured memories by incorporating that place into your décor with

- A framed silhouette of the state
- A flag
- An old license plate
- A framed postcard or map of your hometown
- Photos of your childhood home, school, or other landmarks

Showcase Handwriting From Someone You Love

Handwriting has powerful sentimental value. Frame an envelope that was sent from your grandfather to your grandmother, an old letter, or a collage of old postcards. It will bring a smile to your face after a hectic day and creates an interesting conversation piece.

Know the Story Behind Your Art

Display artwork by a friend or family member—kids' art or artwork from an artist you know or one you've met at an art fair. You'll be reminded of the person who created it every time you see it.

GET A LITTLE RANDOM WITH BOOKSHELVES

You can really draw people in to your bookshelf by mixing things up a little:

- Display some books traditionally—upright, spines out.
- Here and there, interrupt that flow with horizontal stacks of books.
- Use those horizontal stacks as pedestals for photos and small objects of art.
- Mix in heirlooms or items you collect.
- Face out a few visually interesting books to invite people to pick them up.
- Experiment, make it yours, and have fun with it!

DO TRY THIS AT HOME
MIRROR, MIRROR

Make your family or living room the brightest of all by hanging a mirror on the wall. Mirrors reflect light and add the illusion of extra space, so they're great for opening up any small room.

SOFA SPEAK:

What Do You Want Yours To Say?

"RELAX! YOU DESERVE BEAUTY AND COMFORT."

- Throw blanket literally thrown on
- Pillows of different sizes
- Pops of color
- Asymmetrical arrangement

"DON'T YOU DARE MESS ME UP—STAND ALREADY."

- Throw blanket crisply folded
- Pillows all the same size and color
- Perfectly symmetrical arrangement

CREATE A 3 + 1 MANTEL

Whether your style is traditional, modern, or rustic, you can create an appealing mantel or shelf in your living/family room, by following these steps:

ANCHOR the center of the mantel with a large item that has some height: a large framed print or painting, a big wall clock or mirror, a weathered window shutter your grandfather made . . . use your imagination!

BALANCE by placing a group of three items to one side of the anchor and one item on the other side. These balance items could include lamps, pillar candles, and a tall vase filled with fruit, flowers, or branches. Get creative, and experiment with mixing new items with older ones that are meaningful to you.

REST

Home is a refuge from the rush of the world, and a bedroom should be a haven within that haven—the most peaceful and relaxing space of all.

TIDY-UP TUNES:
BEDROOM EDITION

Playlist suggestions to keep you from hiding under the bed:

"I LOVE MY SHIRT"
by Donovan

"GOLDEN SLUMBERS"
by The Beatles

**"DEVIL WITH A
BLUE DRESS ON"**
by Mitch Ryder & The Detroit Wheels

"GOODNIGHT

LAYER YOUR BED FOR LUXURY

A heavenly bed includes

- A top sheet and blanket
- A comforter with duvet cover at the foot of the bed
- Several pillows in varying sizes at the head
- Quilts—especially one that was made by, or once belonged to, someone you love

DO TRY THIS AT HOME

Place a rug or slippers where your feet will hit the floor first thing in the morning.

Soothing, Meaningful Essentials for Your . . .

NIGHTSTAND

- Carafe and water glass
- Good lighting
- A magazine or book (nothing too intense!)

DRESSER

- Photos of family
- A shell from the beach or other lovely memento
- A pretty dish to hold favorite pieces of jewelry when not in use

Soothing, Meaningful Essentials for Your . . .

WALLS

- A soothing paint color
- Photos or other items that remind you of a special time in your life
- Repurposed or antique wall decorations

CORNERS

- A ficus tree to add height or lime tree to add a luscious fragrance

PRETTY UP YOUR CLOSET

When it comes to closet space, don't forget about any blank closet walls or the back of your closet door. You can frame and hang pegboard in either or both of these spots and use it to hang jewelry, scarves, ties, and belts. Bonus: A lot of this stuff is pretty, so you'll actually enjoy seeing it up on your pegboard wall.

BE OUR GUEST

5 Great Things to Have in Your Guest Room

1 A framed corkboard with a "Welcome" sign, Wi-Fi passwords, instructions for using the television and remotes, alarm codes, cell numbers, a list of local coffee shops, a map of the neighborhood, and general information about scheduled events.

2 A guest photo book they can flip through. Before your current guest leaves, take a photo with them to add to the album. Be sure to write your guests' names and the date of their visit.

3 A new toothbrush and toothpaste.

4 A stack of clean fluffy towels just for them.

5 A new thermal tumbler with a lid emblazoned with your city's or favorite team's name. It can be your guest's portable cup to use all weekend, and later, a souvenir of their visit.

BE A KID

A CHILD'S ROOM
IS THE SPACE
WHERE HE PLAYS,
READS, RESTS,
AND DREAMS . . .
WHERE SHE
STUDIES, DRAWS,
DRESSES UP, AND
EXPRESSES
HERSELF.

IT'S ONE
IMPORTANT PLACE!

DO TRY THIS AT HOME

HELP EDIT YOUR CHILD'S BELONGINGS

Get down on the floor together and go paper by paper, book by book, and toy by toy deciding what to keep. Learn more about your child's personality in the process. Some kids are natural editors. Others are borderline hoarders who seem to have deep emotional attachments even to gum wrappers!

Declutter Together Without Meltdowns

- Gather up all the items you want to toss/donate. Allow your child to "save" a few items from the pile and fill a bin with things they absolutely cannot live without.
- Have your child donate some of their old toys to a younger relative or friend so they feel like they're doing something nice for someone else.
- Snap "a photo to remember it by" to help a reluctant child let go of an object that's outlived its usefulness.

When organizing together, never throw in the towel. That would just mean more laundry.

GO FOR A WILD MIX

Matchy-matchy kids rooms can be expensive and inflexible. Here's how to make a wilder, more hodgepodge approach work:

- Use a mix of old, new, vintage, and repurposed pieces in your child's room. The more variety, the more it will look like you meant to do it. (Which you totally did, right?)

- Tie mix-and-match furnishings together with a strong, simple color palette, and it will look even more intentional.

- Add to and change things to fit your child's needs and tastes as he grows. It's so cheap and easy to do when there's no need to match!

TINY TOYS

They're cute. They're collectible. They're almost too small for the human eye to see. Yes, we're talking about TINY TOYS. Whether it's a tiny animal, a tiny grocery item, or an even tinier accessory for those tiny items, here are some zero-effort storage solutions complete with ratings.

1 Hanging Jewelry Organizer

PROS: Allows for sorting. Hang on the back of a closet door, and no one will know you have approximately 4,000 toys in the room!

CONS: Could be more costly than our other solutions. Could require an adult's help to remove from door.

2 Ice Cube Trays

PROS: Allows for great customized storage for kiddos who don't want their animals mixing with their tiny baked goods. Easy to store in a drawer or closet shelf.

CONS: When uncovered, there's a high risk for spilling them all out. When covered, the force of opening the cover could cause spillage. Either way, the probability of crying increases with this option.

3 Tackle Box

PROS: Awesome customizable organization. A see-through tackle box allows kids to more easily find the toys they want to play with. Lower risk of spilling. Portable!

CONS: Maybe not super cute. Have your child decorate it themselves to make it more adorable and less "fishy."

4 Decorative Storage Box

PROS: High on the cuteness factor. Easy to find in stores. Can be left out in a child's room without adding to the clutter.

CONS: It's the Wild West inside that box. No organization whatsoever. Best for kids who don't mind grouping all their toys together!

5 Someone's Nose

PROS: There will never be a pro for this option. This is the worst option ever.

CONS: Emergency room bills, boogers on tiny toys, and every other reason we don't put things in our noses.

BULLETIN BOARD BENEFITS

Here's why a big 'ol bulletin board is a great addition to any child's room:

- It offers a nice, contained space where kids can express themselves and show what they love and what they're proud of without committing long term.

- If you've got a budding collage artist who loves to snip things out of magazines and catalogs, you'll like those scraps a lot better on a bulletin board than on the floor.

- If kids don't learn to use a real, physical bulletin board, then later in life, the whole "pinning" reference on Pinterest will be lost on them.

DO TRY THIS AT HOME

LOFT AND BUNK BEDS

Vertical space is not only your best friend, but also your older child's best friend. A loft bed for a child with her own room or bunk beds for two or more children sharing a room can free up valuable floor real estate. And considering how much time kids spend playing and flopping on the floor, that's priceless. Keep in mind: The American Academy of Pediatrics recommends that kids be at least six years old to sleep on a loft or top bunk, and even then, guard rails are a must.

Hidden Closet Space

In any size closet, think about using the door and walls to store. An over-the-door shoe organizer with pockets can be a great way to to corral:

- Shoes (too obvious?)
- A herd of small stuffed animals
- A band of rogue bouncy balls
- A posse of pencils
- A host of hair clips
- A mob of markers
- A ____ of ____ (Use your imagination. Your child definitely will!)

Wall Shelves

Clear, acrylic wall shelves and ledges can be great for displaying treasured action figures, small dolls, or other prized toys because they allow you to see the entire piece, even from below. Photo ledges, shadow boxes, and type boxes are also fun ways to get favorite collections and meaningful items up on walls, in a place of honor.

THE ART OF MANAGING KIDS' ARTWORK

Manage kids' artwork and school papers in phases:

Short-Term Solutions

BULLETIN BOARD: Display any artwork or school papers your kids are especially proud of on a bulletin board near the spot where they stow shoes and backpacks. As new pieces go up, older ones come down. Most get thrown out after coming down, but a few special favorites get saved.

Long-Term Solutions

KEEPSAKE FILES: At the beginning of the school year, start a file folder for each child and label it with their name and the school year. Into that folder go a select few art masterpieces and other special school papers. Keepsake artwork that's too big for the files goes into a poster tube set aside for each child.

TAKE A PHOTO: If you or your child would like a reminder of a piece that didn't make the keepsake files, then take a photo of it. (Taking photos of artwork can also replace saving and storing any of the artwork itself.) When your child finishes a school year, upload photos and have them printed on a calendar, T-shirt, or photo book for your child or extended family members.

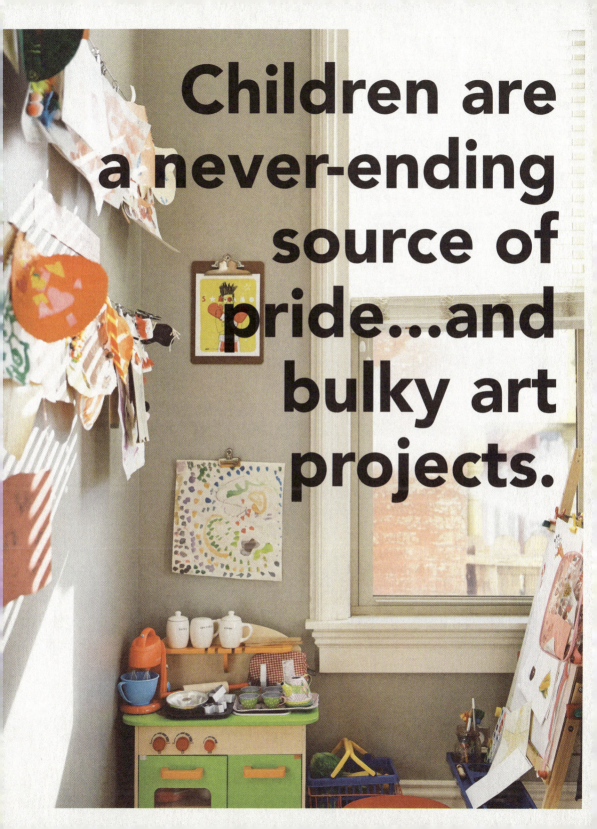

Children are a never-ending source of pride...and bulky art projects.

TIME OUT

- O **Snack**
- O **Drink**
- O **Phone or laptop**

Watch the "Spoonful of Sugar" scene from Mary Poppins online together. Imagine snapping your fingers at kid clutter and watching it magically put itself away. While straightening up may never be that simple, remember the message in the song: Keep the organizing work fun, and it will all go down a little easier.

WHAT KIDS TEACH US

Messy is fun. Being alive is a great reason to laugh. Questions are just as smart as answers. Breakfast is good any time of day. Miracles are everywhere.

CELEBRATE THE HOLIDAYS

Nothing cozies up a home like the holidays.

GO NATURAL

Real greenery and blooms can make a big decorating impact with little effort and require zero need for storage. Don't have a green thumb? No worries—you only have to keep it alive until New Year's! How about

- A fragrant fresh wreath for the front door
- A poinsettia or two
- A single holly branch in a vase

YOUR HOME, YOUR TREE, YOUR WAY.

'TIS THE SEASON TO EMBRACE...CORNY SONGS, TRADITIONS NEW AND OLD, HOMEMADE AND STORE-BOUGHT, THE IDEA OF "GOOD ENOUGH," AND THE PEOPLE YOU LOVE.

Enjoy Gatherings to the Fullest

Getting together with friends and family is why many of us love the holidays in the first place. But it can also translate into a mild case of the dreads if you're not careful.

- If you're hosting, have something planned to keep people entertained. A board game or white-elephant exchange works.

- Let everyone help. Farm out as much as you can. Assign dishes, activities, everything. Taking on too much is a recipe for stress overload.

- If you're a guest, volunteer for what you'd like to contribute or take charge of.

NOTHING SAYS WELCOME TO THE HOLIDAYS LIKE...

- The scent of sugar cookies baking or mulled wine simmering

- A Christmas candy on your guest's pillow or at their place setting

- A basket of slippers to warm feet on cold winter nights

- Twinkle lights along the tops of windows in a child's bedroom

Top 3 Signs Your Holiday Decorations Are Breeding in Storage

1 You notice the lids of your storage containers have taken on a bulging convex shape, thanks to the new baby decorations growing inside.

2 You open your decoration box and discover items you don't recall. Maybe you bought them at a post-holiday sale last year . . . or did you?

3 You open your ornament box and find glass balls in various sizes. The smaller ones are the new generation.

Corral Gift Wrapping Supplies

- During the holidays, use gift bags in different sizes to keep paper, tags, tissue, bows, scissors, and tape handy.

- Hang your gift bags using adhesive-backed wall hooks.

- Loop a bungee cord from the hook around the ends of tall roll wrap that would otherwise fall out.

- You can either leave your wrapping station up year-round or take it down, hooks and all, when the holidays are over.

- For year-round storage, tall containers made for holding wrapping paper and supplies are great. Or, you could be scrappy and repurpose a tall skinny basket, a zippered garment suit bag or even an old trashcan to stash your wrap.

DO TRY THIS AT HOME

UN-DECKING THE HALLS

Divide and Conquer

Assign one person to take down ornaments, another to collect hooks, another to remove lights, and another to place ornaments in their boxes—you're going for the opposite of an assembly line here. Little kids can add an element of madness to the magic, so be sure to assign them age-appropriate tasks if they're going to be a part of the process.

Tuck Away Memories

Make it a habit to tuck in a few little reminders of this year's holiday along with your ornaments: a pretty bow someone gave you, your annual holiday letter and family photo, a meaningful Christmas card you received, even an album of your kids' holiday art. This will spark memories and contribute to the sentimental mood when you open your storage box next year.

Ornament Storage Tips From the Hallmark Archives

Here's how to safely pack and store your treasured Christmas ornaments and other holiday decorations:

- Dust off the ornament or decoration before storing it. If it has any metal hooks, remove those before packing to avoid scratching paint or delicate surfaces.

- Use the original box of the ornament or decoration if you still have it. If you don't have the original box, wrap each ornament and decoration individually. Use acid-free tissue paper for metal and paper ornaments. Use cotton batting (sold at craft and fabric stores) for glass or more fragile decorations and ornaments.

- Store decorations in boxes or plastic containers that closely fit the size of the decoration. The size of the container is more important than what the container is made of. You want a little room around the item so you can add tissue paper or cotton batting around the sides. Partitioned boxes (like egg cartons for small ornaments or boxes used to hold bottles of wine for larger decorations) are best for storing several individual items. Use plenty of padding between each item.

- After you've packed your decorations, store the containers in a place that doesn't get too hot or too humid.

- If you stack your containers, put the heaviest containers on the bottom.

House lights twinkle, "Welcome." Trees in windows add their glow. The holidays shine bright and merry everywhere you go.

SPECIAL THANKS TO
DARREN ABBOTT
JODI ABBOTT
APRIL BLACK
WILL BROWN
MEGHAN CRAIG
RENEE DANIELS
SANDI DEVENNEY
TOMMY DONOHO
JENNIFER DREILING
JOSH DUSEL
CAROLINA FERNANDEZ

JENNIFER FUJITA
LINDSEY HAMILTON
ASHLEY HARMS
ALFRED JONES
JANE KORTRIGHT
DEAN KUBE
TINA NEIDLEIN
ANDY NEWCOM
TUESDAY SPRAY
KATHERINE STANO
ASHLEY TRAVALENTGER

If you have enjoyed this book
or it has touched your life in some way,
we would love to hear from you.

Please send your comments to:
Hallmark Book Feedback
P.O. Box 419034
Mail Drop 100
Kansas City, MO 64141

Or e-mail us at:

booknotes@hallmark.com